BEST A NEW ZEALAND COMPENDIUM

BE

ST

A NEW ZEALAND COMPENDIUM

COMPILED BY ELLA GRIFFITHS

AWA PRESS

First edition published in 2004 by
Awa Press, PO Box 11-416, Wellington, New Zealand

National Library of New Zealand Cataloguing-in-Publication Data
Best: A New Zealand Compendium / compiled by Ella Griffiths
ISBN 0-9582509-2-8
1. Popular culture—New Zealand. 2. National characteristics,
New Zealand. 3. New Zealand—Description and travel
I. Griffiths, Ella, 1978-
306.0993—dc 22

Designed by Sarah Maxey, Wellington
Typeset by Archetype, Wellington
Printed by Astra Print, Wellington

www.awapress.com

CONTENTS

OTHER BOOKS FROM AWA PRESS

Embracing the Dragon:
A woman's journey along the Great Wall of China
POLLY GREEKS

The Miss Tutti Frutti Contest:
Travel Tales of the South Pacific
GRAEME LAY

Magnificent Obsessions:
The people who saved Wellington's great places and how they did it
MARY VARNHAM with photographs by ANNELIES VAN DER POEL

Mouthful: Simple & Stunning Party Food
DANIELLE BOWATER with photographs by SHAUN CATO-SYMONDS

THE GINGER SERIES
How to Watch a Game of Rugby SPIRO ZAVOS
How to Gaze at the Southern Stars RICHARD HALL
How to Listen to Pop Music NICK BOLLINGER
How to Pick a Winner MARY MOUNTIER
How to Play a Guitar ZOLTON ZAVOS
How to Drink a Glass of Wine JOHN SAKER

FROM THE PUBLISHER

Welcome to *Best: A New Zealand Compendium*. And welcome, too, to Awa Press, a new, wholly independent, New Zealand publishing company.

Our goal is to publish and promote the best of modern non-fiction by New Zealand and overseas authors. We are committed to excellent writing, beautiful design and state-of-the-art production.

Best is one of our first books and so a cause for celebration. We didn't want to bring you the usual, obvious things that make New Zealand a great place to live in and visit. We wanted to tap into the eclectic, the unexpected and the amazing. Our contributors came to the party in style. We thank them all for their enthusiasm, their generosity and their confidence in us. Enormous thanks are due also to Ella Griffiths, who worked indefatigably to compile *Best*.

If, after having read this book, you, the reader, wish to argue the toss about any of these Bests, or suggest some Bests of your own, we would love to hear from you. Just write to Awa Press, PO Box 11-416, Wellington or email us, best@awapress.co.nz.

And look out for *Best 2* – your views and ideas may just feature.

Mary Varnham
June 2004

BEST ADRENALINE RUSH

Night climb to erupting crater

Geoff Mackley

Striking out for the summit of Mount Ruapehu at three in the morning seemed like a good idea at the time. I was covering the volcano's eruption for TV3 and, in keeping with my usual drive to get closer and better pictures than everyone else, I decided the only way to do that was to get up to the summit.

No helicopter pilot would fly me there and there was a ten-kilometre police cordon around the mountain. However it was impossible to cordon off a whole mountain. Having spent my life climbing and tramping, it was no big deal to go across country through the bush and then climb the mountain.

Arriving at the top at daybreak, I had to dodge fridge-sized rocks falling around me. The resulting footage, and the uproar about my climbing an

erupting volcano, made headlines around the world and launched me into a full-time career of documenting and filming volcanic eruptions and other natural disasters. Since this 1995 event, I have been to over thirty eruptions all over the world, from Siberia to the Caribbean.

GEOFF MACKLEY is a New Zealand free-lance filmmaker and photographer. Passionate about nature in its most violent moods, he has filmed hurricanes in Mexico, typhoons in Japan, tornadoes in Kansas, floods in Indonesia and hundreds of other extreme events. His pictures regularly feature on the world's major television networks and he is the subject of the 2004 Discovery Channel series Dangerman.

BEST MUSIC VIDEO

Stand Up, Scribe

Jaquie Brown

JAQUIE BROWN *is a presenter for music television channel C4. She hosted TV2's live music show* Space *for three years and has had over ten years in radio. 'I am a girl, I love New Zealand and my star sign is Libra.'*

When I first saw *Stand Up* I was glued to the screen. Never before had a New Zealand artist been smart enough to reference other musicians in a song, let alone feature them in the video. Like *Where's Wally?* there were endless sessions of spotting Nesian Mystik, Blindspott, the D4, P-Money, DJ Sirvere, and the countless excitable extras all pushing for their moment of fame.

This video, directed by Chris Graham, propelled Scribe on to the fame superhighway. The single of the song went to number one in the New Zealand charts, and Scribe's debut album *The Crusader* simultaneously took the top album spot – a double that made New Zealand music history.

Honourable mentions must go to Dave Dobbyn's *Loyal* and *Don't* by Anika Moa. *Don't* is a simple, beautiful animation. Inspired by an idea by Paul

McLaney, aka Gramsci, it features a man holding a rope which leads off into the sky. A woman is doing a tightrope-walking act on the rope. With the help of choreographer France Herve, the director, Edward Davis, created a surreal collage of reality and fairy tale. 'While France mimed the tightrope routine on the floor, I filmed the video in one continuous shot, walking all around her, then up a stairway to a catwalk,' Davis later explained. Using after-effects trickery he then replaced the background with images from around the country, including aerial shots of Wellington and views of Mount Ngauruhoe.

As for *Loyal*, you cannot *not* love this video, shot simply and featuring the legend that is Dave Dobbyn, wearing a tremendous mullet and a sumptuous woollen, multi-coloured, 1980s' sweater.

BEST ICE CREAM

Deep South Vanilla and Kapiti Fig & Honey

Kay McMath

New Zealand ice cream is among the best in the world – the country's dairying heritage means we have some of the finest ingredients available – and one of the best of the best is Deep South's Vanilla. Deep South, based in Invercargill, is a family-run business which prides itself on using local ingredients, from fresh cream to berry fruit. In their wonderful vanilla ice cream, a medal winner for more than three years at the annual Ice Cream Awards, the fresh-cream flavour blends well with the sweetness and the delicate hint of vanilla. The Simon family who own Deep South are life members of the New Zealand Ice Cream Manufacturers Association and their long experience shines through.

Kapiti's Fig & Honey, also an award winner, combines the wild flavour of New Zealand honey

with the gentle sweetness of figs. Both flavours remain clearly recognisable, and are enhanced by the creamy texture. The idea came from a traditional dessert menu where figs and honey were typically served with custard and cream. A simple transition from cream and custard to ice cream and *voila* – sheer indulgence!

KAY McMATH *is a judge in the New Zealand Ice Cream Awards. She spent twelve years in the New Zealand dairy industry, evaluating ingredients and products for export. She now works as a consultant, assisting food companies to develop high-quality consumer products for both local and export markets.*

BEST DOC HUT

Cupola Basin Hut

Lyn Jowett

This inviting little hut in Nelson Lakes National Park sits just above the beech tree-line. Originally built for chamois research in the 1960s, it is flooded with light from an unusually large window. There are wonderful views over the Cupola Basin to the majestic Mount Hopeless.

Getting there is a day's expedition. From the head of Lake Rotoiti it is a pleasant five hours' walk to John Tait Hut, then another two or three hours up to the Cupola Basin, following the Travers River and the Cupola Creek. The hut is situated on the edge of what looks like an enormous basin of rock (hence the name), now covered in grasses and alpine flora. Around the edges are mountains on the higher western sides, and beech forest below.

On a May visit to the hut, our first ascent was a pleasant, non-technical climb on the north face

of Cupola – the perfect warm-up before tackling the more serious snow and rock climb of the south ridge of Mount Hopeless. On this we had to rope up for some of the chimneys, but mostly it was an exhilarating free climb to the silent summit.

In the chill of the evenings we would return to our haven, light the coal fire and revel in our climbing successes. After six days of perfect weather, good company and great climbs, we returned to our city lives with spirits rejuvenated, vowing to come back again to relive our primitive emotions – thirst and hunger, fear and triumph.

LYN JOWETT *is the director of Bushwise Women, which provides adventure holidays for women. She has more than thirty years' experience in outdoor pursuits.*

BEST CAFÉ

The Store

Wanda Passadore

If you're passing through Hobbiton (the former Matamata) some time, crunch over the railway line to the Workman's Café. The art deco decor is a stand-out and there is probably not another eating place in New Zealand, or indeed the world, that boasts a corset as a food come-on.

Wellington, meanwhile, sports Caffe L'Affare, run by the genial Jeff Kennedy. This virtual inventor of New Zealand's café culture clings to the quaint idea that the best food is fresh, lovingly cooked and blissfully unadorned.

The Chez in Nelson has metamorphosised from the legendary Chez Eelco, which used to claim to have the first espresso machine in New Zealand. Its footpath tables are the closest you can come to Europe without actually choking on Gauloise.

All of these places will give you good coffee, people to watch and satisfying food. But none will do for your soul what The Store will. Located on State Highway One in Kekerengu, Marlborough, this spacious, relaxed café and its delicious deck gaze out over the wild Pacific from a place formerly known as the middle of nowhere. Now it's definitely somewhere.

WANDA PASSADORE *has to have a mega latté by 10 a.m. each day.*

BEST JAZZ ENSEMBLE

Anthony Donaldson and
The Village Idiots

Jeff Henderson

JEFF HENDERSON *is artistic director of the Wellington International Jazz Festival and the Bomb the Space Festival of Experimental Music, and runs Wellington performance venue Happy. An improvising musician, his main instrument is the saxophone. He has performed and recorded throughout Europe, the USA and Australasia.*

The Village Idiots have created some of the most exciting and diverse New Zealand music I have had the pleasure of hearing in recent years. Drummer and bandleader Anthony Donaldson sculpts fascinating musical forms informed by his thirty years as a cutting-edge improvising musician and his wide-ranging musical tastes. Everything from Kurosawa soundtracks to death metal to psychedelic rock to early jazz is used as inspiration and source material.

In Wellington in the early 1990s, I would go and listen to groups such as Bung Notes, The Razor Blades, Doodletown Boptet and, occasionally, a Primitive Art Group reunion. The influence of these groups and their collective of musicians is emerging as one of the most important periods in the development of New Zealand improvised music.

As jazz seems to become more and more institutionalised and conservative, creative improvisers such as Anthony Donaldson are becoming more prolific, and determined to counter the gentrification of a vibrant art form with visionary projects and an uncompromising attitude.

In The Village Idiots' show *Seven Samurai*, two warriors armed with razor-sharp swords emerged from the wings to take centre stage. A menacing ostinato figure was built up by the band, and the warriors created an almost unbearable tension with minimal movement and false threats. As the music peaked, one samurai attacked, and was slain with a quick, precise blow from the other – a fitting ode to the death of jazz, and the life of new, original New Zealand music.

BEST NATIVE TREE FOR A SMALL GARDEN

Ti Kouka, Cabbage Tree

Sue McLean

Twenty years ago, still in the grip of the English garden tradition, I rejected the ordinary, messy cabbage tree. Since then I've been seduced by this evocative national treasure, with its brilliant architectural form, its dramatic green blades thrusting from slender stems and its huge, creamy-white bouquets held aloft in late spring.

The cabbage tree fits into any garden and grows almost anywhere. It claims little territory and doesn't mind if conditions are sunny, shady, salty or soggy. Ironically, given its historic neglect by New Zealand gardeners, it has long been adored by their English and Mediterranean counterparts for its beauty, versatility and hardiness.

There are five native species: Cordyline australis, the most widespread and hardy; C. banksii, ideal for small gardens; C. kaspar,

whose tropical luxuriance is well worth protecting from frost; C. indivisa, the broad-leafed mountain cabbage tree which needs high altitude and cool summers; and C. pumilo, which grows no more than a metre and loves a dry rock garden.

My own small Auckland garden looks out on a reserve of pohutukawa, karaka, puriri and titoki. From upstairs, the upper Waitemata shimmers through the billowing green of these aristocrats.

But it's the fantastic heads of cabbage trees, leaping from nowhere and thrusting their way through the canopy, which really excite me. At sunset their spiky silhouettes pierce the sky, the flowers turn pink and the fragrance lets loose. For this I will gladly gather the often cursed withered blades and bundle the spent beauty of our marvellous ti kouka.

SUE McLEAN *is a leading Auckland garden designer, and partner in McLean Landscapes.*

BEST PLAY

Blue Sky Boys

Denis Welch

DENIS WELCH *is a feature writer for the* New Zealand Listener, *a poet, and a former Wellington theatre critic and judge of the Chapman Tripp Theatre Awards. His novel,* Human Remains, *was published in 1999.*

Cramped, poky, run on a shoestring and entirely lacking in glitz, Wellington's Bats Theatre has always had a crucible-like quality: just about anything gets thrown into the theatrical fire and sometimes pure gold emerges. So it was, on June 16, 1990, that Ken Duncum's play *Blue Sky Boys* opened.

The idea was brilliantly simple: what if, on the night the Beatles played Wellington in 1964, the Everly Brothers were also in town? And not only in town, but at the nadir of their career, reduced to performing in the Buffalo Hall — the very premises shared by Bats?

The result was electrifying. With hair pompadoured to extraordinary heights, Tim Balme and Michael Galvin gave stunning performances as Don and Phil, acting out the brothers' bitter sibling rivalry

while singing and playing all their great hits. And, by connecting us to the Everlys through two teenage girls who had wound up at the wrong show, Duncum got Kiwi cultural cringe squaring off against international stardom.

BEST GOLF COURSE

Paraparaumu Beach Links and Kauri Cliffs Golf Course

Michael Campbell

MICHAEL CAMPBELL, *of Maori (Ngati Ruanui and Nga Rauru) and Scottish descent, started golf caddying for his father, Tom, at Titahi Golf Club. By ten he had joined the club himself, and by twelve he had a handicap of 11. Michael Campbell turned professional in 1993. In 1999 he held off Tiger Woods to win the Johnnie Walker Classic in Taiwan and by the end of 2000 was ranked 14th in the world.*

I have two favourite courses in New Zealand, Paraparaumu and Kauri Cliffs. These are completely different.

Paraparaumu is a challenging seaside course, which reminds me of the links courses in Scotland. In my younger days I lived close to Paraparaumu and I have fond memories of playing there as an amateur, notwithstanding the success I had there in 2000 as a professional.

Kauri Cliffs in Northland is one of the most picturesque courses in the world, with unbelievable views of the nearby islands and ocean. The scenery really blows you away. I have affiliation with the course as the 'attached professional' and visit every time I am back in New Zealand.

BEST BLUE CHEESE

Mercer Ewes' Blue

Juliet Harbutt

New Zealand makes some excellent blue cheeses but the one that stands out is Mercer Ewes' Blue. This is made as a seven-kilogram round, then turned into an oblong 'brick' which looks very rustic, demanding to be eaten.

The exceptional flavour – intensely herbaceous, with overtones of dark chocolate, sweet, burnt caramel and roasted onions – comes from a combination of the grass the sheep graze on, the complexity and sweetness of their milk, and the art of cheese-maker, Albert Alferink.

The texture is quite dry, yet melt-in-the-mouth. And, unlike many blues, this cheese is not gritty but quite hard: it breaks in chunks, rather than crumbles or flakes.

Ewes' Blue has a delicious balance of salt to the richness of

the milk, and its blue-green-grey mould is scattered in chunky blotches, like gorse on a hillside. If I never had another blue cheese, I would die happy.

Mercer Cheese has a wonderful shop just off the main Auckland-to-Hamilton road. Here they sell Ewes' Blue, along with other, mostly Dutch-style, cheeses.

Cheese lovers ignore this emporium at their peril. From floor to ceiling, every nook and cranny boasts magnificent cheeses, each shouting, 'Pick me!'

JULIET HARBUTT, *a champion for handcrafted cheese, created both the New Zealand and British Cheese Awards and Festivals. She is co-author of* The World Encyclopedia of Cheese, *the author of* Cheese *and a columnist for* New Zealand House and Garden.

BEST PARK

Grey Lynn Park

Mary Varnham

It was a hot Auckland summer day, one of those where the sweat runs in rivulets down your face and you would kill for a drink, and a tree to swig it under. My son, a musician who had recently moved to Auckland, had suggested we meet at Grey Lynn Park, where a festival was happening. I hadn't been to the park before but finding it wasn't hard: streams of barely-clad people were coursing in the general direction, clutching sunhats, chillibins and children.

Nothing, though, prepared me for the scene that unfurled when I came though the entrance and over the rise: a shimmering swathe of grass and trees, strewn with a crazy-paving of people, awnings and umbrellas. Music pulsated and the air was saturated with the smell of food. As a campaigner for inner-city parks, I had died and gone to heaven.

Like many great public open spaces, Grey Lynn Park came about through citizen agitation. When Surrey Hills estate, then Auckland's largest subdivision, was developed in 1883, the developers resisted calls for a public park. However a large area proved too wet and steep for housing and finally, in 1914, after continuing public pressure, it was drained and flattened.

Today Grey Lynn Park covers 10.5 hectares. It has three playing fields, two children's playgrounds, a basketball court, a sculpture park and many other facilities. The fabulous Grey Lynn Park Festival happens every November and has even spawned its own CD.

MARY VARNHAM, *writer and publisher, founded Chaffers Park – Make It Happen!, a campaign for a waterfront park in Wellington's inner city, in 1997. The city council fought the park for years but in 2002 bowed to citizen pressure and allocated $18 million to its creation.*

BEST REGGAE BAND

Dread, Beat & Blood

Nandor Tanczos

NANDOR TANCZOS, co-founder of the 'One Love' Waitangi Day reggae celebrations, was elected to the New Zealand parliament in 1999 as a Green Party candidate. He is New Zealand's first dreadlocked, Ras Tafarian MP. He prefers roots, ragga and churchical Nyabhingi chants.

Blasting out from the Rasta yards of Porirua, Dread, Beat & Blood was a crucial voice in the first wave of Aotearoa reggae. Along with Herbs, Sticks N Shanty and Mana, the band defined Pacific reggae. Its sweet sounds were distinct from the dry and heavy Jamaican and English rhythms, but carried an anti-colonial shout of anger that spread the message of Ras Tafari.

Tracks such as 'Love in the Ghetto' and 'Colonial Law', from the album *Tribute to a Friend*, highlighted the struggle for justice and dignity in the face of racism and oppression. David Grace and the crew demonstrated Ras Tafari livity and overstanding in a way unmatched by many of the more popular and slick reggae musicians of today. Maximum RASpect.

DREAD, BEAT & BLOOD

TRIBUTE TO A FRIEND

BEST BEER

Captain Cooker Manuka

Geoff Griggs

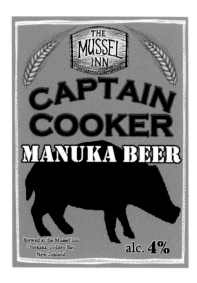

A few miles beyond Takaka, in the settlement of Onekaka, Andrew Dixon (pictured) and Jane Dixon have for ten years run the rustic Mussel Inn pub and microbrewery. In a tiny (350 litre) brew house, ace brewer Reuben Lee conjures up a superb range of craft beers that are sold exclusively at the pub.

Flagship of the Mussel Inn beers is undoubtedly the remarkable Captain Cooker Manuka Beer. Using manuka shoots and leaves to aromatise and flavour the beer, and only a tiny amount of hops for a hint of bitterness, Lee creates a sweetish, perfumy, spicy amber brew which delights the senses.

GEOFF GRIGGS *has been described as New Zealand's leading beer guru. An Englishman, he arrived in Wellington in 1995 after twenty years as a video journalist for BBC Television News, a career which saw him learning about beer in many parts of Europe, Russia and the*

United States. He became an activist for
real ale, and a judge at British beer
festivals.

   Since moving to New Zealand, Geoff
has run beer-tasting events, written on
beer and trained staff for The Malthouse,
a specialist beer bar.

BEST KIWIANA

Horopito Motors

David McGill

DAVID McGILL *has been fossicking in Kiwiland all his life. His owl collection started with a brass thermometer funded from his first job at age twelve, tying up 850 tomato plants for twelve shillings and sixpence. Now he has over three hundred owls, plus clocks, dolls, pharmaceutical jars, musical instruments, and notes on more odd collectors, like the Wageners (late of Houhora and Matakohe), the Paeroa canal, Jack Wilson's Orepuki Chinese bottle collection … you name it. Save everything!*

I came across it first on paper, when my *Evening Post* colleague Grant Tilly said he had something larger than the cute old Wellington houses he drew and I wrote about. He had got away to his Ohakune bach but had taken his pencils with him and here was the result, a thrilling triptych to rival the size of the Monet's *Water Lilies*.

Crikey dick! It was a stupendous rendering of a massive wreckers' yard. Hang about! This rusting pile of cars on cars knocked five years' worth of Antiques Roadshow into a Pommie hat. The cars may have emanated from Britland and the US of A, but we'd kept them. We Kiwis are great hoarders.

Turned out this was a world-famous *vintage* car wreckers. Grant knew heaps about the old Willys, Hispano Stutzs, Cords

28 / 29   BEST A NEW ZEALAND COMPENDIUM

and Studebakers, and the kind of pit-bull V8s Robert Mitchum used to moonlight down B-grade movie roads in Kentucky. I was into my Rover 95 and up that way quick smart. Oh, glorious junk! Forget the gleaming collection in the Southward Car Museum, this was the real thing – authentically rusting, treasured junk piles.

The Rover negotiated the country's C-grade roads for my first book, *Ghost Towns of New Zealand*, without ending up in Horopito. But it deserves to, eventually. Later, the movie *Smash Palace* blew the place's relatively secret status. Despite the fame, though, it remains a real dinkum, unspoiled, un-made-over Kiwi effort. Good on it.

BEST INDEPENDENT CINEMA

The Paramount

Miles Buckingham

MILES BUCKINGHAM *is a film critic. He watches around 140 films a year and talks about them on the wireless, an archaic, picture-less medium.*

I first discovered Wellington's Paramount in its flea-pit days during the mid 1980s. It had a repertory season on, conveniently in the middle of the school holidays, and the staff neglected to ask for ID from eager schoolboys wanting to see the R18 German art-house classic *The Tin Drum*.

Needless to say, my film education picked up with this discovery and, within a matter of a year or so, I was driving into town every Sunday for the Paramount's double feature, regardless of what it was.

In those days I knew which seats to avoid due to their flea infestation. Thankfully, in recent years the Paramount has undergone a thorough refurbishment. It continues to screen a diverse selection of films, both in its general programme and in the numerous film festivals it hosts.

BEST POEM

'Home Thoughts'

Miranda Harcourt

MIRANDA HARCOURT *has won awards as an actor, short film director and stage director, and gained national attention with her stage and screen work with prison inmates. Head of the acting programme at Toi Whakaari: New Zealand Drama School, she is married to writer and film-maker Stuart McKenzie, with whom she has two children.*

There is no such thing as the best … of anything. There is only the marvellous prospect of conflict over different opinions about the best.

One of the poems that makes me laugh the best is Jenny Bornholdt's 'Then Murray Came'. Using the rhythm of everyday speech and an eye for telling detail, she imbues a seemingly unremarkable event – the breakdown of an old car – with warmth and humour.

But when I was growing up the poem that gave me the best kick in the pants was 'Home Thoughts' by Denis Glover.

At the age of ten I was lucky enough to have a teacher who went through my first essay in a new school with a red pen, mercilessly scoring

out the colonialist flavour
I had picked up from an
unrelenting diet of Alison
Uttley, Enid Blyton and Joyce
Lancaster Brisley.

Under this teacher's tutelage
'stream' became 'creek'
and 'forest' became 'bush'.
She introduced us to poetry
written by and for New
Zealanders – and 'Home
Thoughts' struck a chord as
I woke up to my own
cultural cringe.

The poet's ironic tone as
he writes about developing
indigenous culture, and
about where we draw our
inspiration, seems prescient.

But even Denis Glover may
have found it sobering that,
fifty or so years later, we are
still fighting to make our own
mark, tell our own stories
and value the sound of our
own voice.

I do not dream of Sussex downs
or quaint old England's
quaint old towns –
I think of what may yet be seen
in Johnsonville or Geraldine.

DENIS GLOVER

BEST GREAT WALK

Heaphy Track

Craig Potton

It's the variety that makes New Zealand's Great Walks such an extraordinary natural wealth. It's difficult to choose a best one because you can't compare volcanic to greywacke landscapes.

The Heaphy Track in Kahurangi National Park, though, is a personal favourite of mine. It passes through lowland and mountain beech forests, an alpine peneplain with limestone outcrops that have many endemic species, and a luxuriant coastal forest full of palms and lianes. There is a variety of bird life, including kiwi on the upland downs. It's not a physically demanding walk but there's a huge sense of wilderness in being out there for three to four days.

CRAIG POTTON *is a photographer, publisher and political activist, who climbs in the hills and goes surfing in his spare time.*

BEST PINOT NOIR

Fromm La Strada 1994 Pinot Noir

Bob Campbell

BOB CAMPBELL *is the author of the* New Zealand Wine Annual, *group wine editor of ACP Media and a senior wine judge.*

The best New Zealand pinot noir I have ever tasted is Fromm La Strada 1994 Pinot Noir, en magnum. Marlborough's Fromm Winery does not enter wine competitions. Nor does it send review samples to writers. So, although I taste over five thousand wines each year, this particular gem had escaped my clutches until, a year after its release, I attended a charity wine auction.

I normally avoid auctions because I have an impulsive nature and occasionally regret the consequences of hasty action. In this case, however, I was the auctioneer. When the magnum of Fromm Pinot Noir was offered I made a generous opening bid. The crowd must have sensed my determination. No further bids were made. I owned the wine and my credit card was deeper in debt.

LA STRADA

— PINOT NOIR —

MARLBOROUGH · FROMM

CONTAINS PRESERVATIVE [220]

HUMM

19
94

PRODUCED AND BOTTLED BY FROMM WINERY, GODFREY
ROAD, BLENHEIM, NEW ZEALAND. ALC/VOL 13,0% 1500 ML

There are two sorts of people in this world: hedonists and hoarders. I am a hedonist. I am no more capable of keeping great wine than Dr Don Brash is of dropping his trousers at late-night parties in the Beehive. So, two weeks after I bought the magnum, I drank it – with the help of several good friends and an exquisitely cooked, butterflied leg of lamb. The wine was glorious. As we sat in stunned silence we could hear the faint notes of a celestial choir singing the Hallelujah chorus.

BEST ALBUM BY A SOLO ARTIST

Get Up With The Sun

Nick Bollinger

Corben Simpson was the first singer who gave me goose bumps. When I was a schoolboy in the early '70s I heard him often, both solo and with Blerta, Bruno Lawrence's acid-anarchist circus.

His voice was a little like Van Morrison's but lighter and more supple, with a couple of extra octaves. He would begin a song intensely, at what you assumed was the top of his range, then astonishingly soar upwards. Sometimes he would discard the lyrics and weave wordless, improvised melodies – a human trumpet.

He was fearless. One night I saw him opening solo for Split Enz. He ordered the sound man to turn off the microphone, and his voice, unamplified, filled Wellington's Opera House. At a festival in Ngaruawahia he took his clothes off; he felt more comfortable singing naked, he said.

CORBEN SIMPSON

The last time I heard him was at Bruno Lawrence's tangi. He looked derelict but the voice was still pure. He hasn't made an album since *Get Up With The Sun*, but with angry rants like 'No Trespassing', reinvented standards like 'Mr Bojangles', wordless excursions like 'What??' and idyllic anthems like 'Running To The Sea', this classic work still shocks and inspires me.

NICK BOLLINGER *is a critic, broadcaster and musician. He writes regularly for the* New Zealand Listener, *presents the music review programme* The Sampler *on National Radio, and plays bass for the Windy City Strugglers.*

BEST DIVE SPOT

Northern Arch, Poor Knights Islands

Wade Doak

It's a perfect ocean day as I fin across to an archway in a dark promontory. Powerful ocean swells pulse through a keyhole in a cliff that rises fifteen storeys from coral sands, continuing above the water to a saw-tooth ridge. I up-end and meet the current coursing through this sumptuously adorned sea corridor.

Looking towards the surface, I'm in an aviation dream. Twelve metres above me a squadron of forty white delta undersides gleam in the light of my movie camera. Beneath the nearest stingray, five gill slits open and shut like air vents, on either side of a gummy, shell-crunching mouth. Whiptails stream astern, flattened vertically near the end for steerage. Rear fins, like aircraft wing-flaps, act as brakes for stalls and turns.

I gaze below. Another forty barb-tailed black diamonds are

stacked level upon level: giant birds from another planet. Their undulating ocean wings ride the sea wind in static horizontal flight, diminishing size by size down into the dim depths.

At my level, one short-tail stingray pirouettes. Fibrillations run along its wing skirts in high frequency waves. A tiny eye swivels in front of the upper gill cavity. I am being surveyed …

We're out at the Northern Arch. For me this place has become not just a favourite dive spot, but a gateway for understanding the ocean.

WADE DOAK *was a language teacher with a passion for diving, when, in 1969, while diving on a shipwreck, he discovered a stash of coins. Treasure salvage allowed him to devote his life to studying and photographing 'the blue planet' and he has published 20 books about the ocean and its inhabitants. He also worked on the television series* Wild South *and* Deep Blue: A South Pacific Odyssey.

BEST RADIO BREAKFAST SHOW

Morning Report

David Hill

You mean there's more than one radio breakfast show? Of course there are. All across the commercial spectrum, cretinous combinations called Haylee 'n' Robbee or Jodee 'n' Barnee run shows where they play 'jokes' on listeners by phoning them and lying to them. Or they seize upon the fact it's National Penis Day to slosh through double entendres that make you pray no intelligent life-forms near Alpha Centauri are judging the human race from *these* radio emissions.

But for grown-ups there's only one breakfast show – National Radio's *Morning Report*, usually (at the time of writing) with Geoff Robinson and Sean Plunket. It's three hours with almost no National Radio music (praise the Lord), but a chorus of nationwide and worldwide reports. *Morning Report* has interviews, not interrogations: the evening show,

Checkpoint, over-indulges itself with those. And it has news, news, news – Rural News, Sports News, Business News, Pacific News, Traffic News, Mana News, News Bulletins, News Headlines, even News-Papers. By the end you feel informed, in touch and in control. Then you get to work …

DAVID HILL _is a radio reviewer for the_ New Zealand Listener, _and a full-time writer. His stories, plays and novels for teenagers have been published in twelve countries and eight languages._

BEST BOUTIQUE HOTEL

Awaroa Lodge

Shelley-Maree Cassidy

SHELLEY-MAREE CASSIDY *is the author of* A Place to Stay – Hotels of New Zealand *and several other books about interesting places to stay around the world, from Africa to America. Her great-grandparents were among the first hoteliers in New Zealand.*

In May 2003 my mother died. A few days later I had to go to Awaroa Lodge in Abel Tasman National Park to research a book I was writing on New Zealand hotels. I was wrapped in sadness; the world felt and looked grey. But on the boat ride there the stunningly fine day broke through. The sea was dark blue and glittery, the beaches clear and golden, the bush richly green. Everything looked fresh and sharply bright.

As there's no jetty at Awaroa Bay, I had to wade through water to reach the shore. It was cold and well above my ankles – a small shock of arrival. After a short walk through bush, the lodge came into view, nestled against hills, surrounded by trees.

Awaroa Lodge is peaceful, and in a beautiful spot. Although it is set away from the beach, the sound of the surf travels to it.

Being there gave me back some
energy – and a gentle reminder in
my grieving that there was still
much to be glad about.

BEST NOVEL

Coal Flat

Tilly Lloyd

The diagnosticians of New Zealand literature seem to pinpoint John Mulgan's *Man Alone*, and who is a bookseller to disagree? But Bill Pearson's *Coal Flat* provided me with one of those profound reading experiences we all like so much, slumped in a hot family crib in Matakaea/Shag Point, half a mile (as it was then) above the miners in the black tunnels that stretched out under the Pacific.

I think its effect (although this could be an overlay) was that it was about a town, rather than a person. The book is out of print, and 'OP' always has that unfair feel of redundancy about it. However social critic and Marxist Jean Devanny's *Butcher Shop*, banned in 1926, received an anti-obscurity reprint and so too may *Coal Flat*.

More recently the 'memorable-ness' or 'resonatingness' of

Coal Flat occurred with three contemporary novels, which I believe will last, or at least go into literati's 'best of' lists. In the mid '80s it seemed everyone was talking about Keri Hulme's *the bone people*. While waiters burst madly around us, we regulars of Java restaurant grouped tightly under the TV in the kitchen to watch Keri and the Spiral Collective pick up the big prize on Booker night.

Elizabeth Knox's *The Vintner's Luck* seemed to re-frame New Zealand literature and I bet, and lost, money on it picking up that big prize too. And Lloyd Jones' brilliantly durable *The Book of Fame* has had possibly the most reach into New Zealand households, capturing – here within a rugby team rather than Pearson's town – all the understated social glue we hanker to understand.

TILLY LLOYD *is the manager of Unity Books Wellington and a past judge of the Montana New Zealand Book Awards.*

BEST PRIVATE GARDEN TO VISIT

Ayrlies

Maggie Barry

MAGGIE BARRY *was a current affairs broadcaster on National Radio for ten years before leaving in 1992 to present and co-produce a television gardening programme.* Maggie's Garden Show *ran for twelve years, during which time Maggie and her team visited and filmed more than 2000 New Zealand gardens.*

Bev McConnell and her late husband Malcolm dreamed of making a large country garden on their land in Howick, Auckland. Today, more than 30 years after the first paddock was fenced off, thousands of visitors a year enjoy their vision.

A hillside garden, Ayrlies follows the land's natural contours, and the plantings and water features go with the flow. But these are no accidents of nature. The apparently effortless colour and texture combinations are the result of meticulous planning by a consummate plantswoman with a fine arts background.

Ayrlies is a garden that really does have it all. But even though it's breathtaking, it's never overwhelming. It's a place where you can kick off your shoes and walk barefoot on the lush, expansive lawns. It also possesses that elusive quality, a sense of occasion. On a balmy, late summer evening there is no better place to be than on the lawn with 700 opera fans and their picnic hampers, hearing voices lifted passionately in song.

For me, Ayrlies is the quintessential New Zealand garden. It doesn't try to be Italian or English or French; it's totally at ease with its own identity. It couldn't have been made anywhere else and it belongs to this land. For Bev, the ten acres of rolling hills are her turangawaewae, her place to stand. And if there's ever time to sit, she may be found in her Scottish-inspired sitooteree, a wee building with such a low-slung roof you have no choice but to sit and rest a while – the ideal spot for an indefatigable gardener to contemplate her ever-evolving vision of paradise.

BEST SPORTS COMMENTATOR

Winston McCarthy

Keith Quinn

I first became aware of Winston McCarthy's distinctive radio rugby commentary voice when my father used to do impersonations of it around the family dinner table on long winter nights. This was back in the 1950s, when there was no television, and radio was king.

Winston made the first of his famous broadcasting tours accompanying the Kiwi army rugby team around Britain in 1945/46, a tour which rekindled the game after the horrors of World War II. Winston's loud, excitable commentary was completely opposite to the BBC's dignified, old-school-tie style. When British radio audiences heard Winston they soon asked the BBC for his commentaries rather than their own.

Winston became a powerful figure in New Zealand sport. The radio audience *had* to believe his opinions as there was no comparison with television pictures. It was said he influenced the All Black selectors, such was his enthusiasm for favourite players.

Many a dull match was made exciting by the way Winston talked it up. When a kick for goal was being taken from the other side of the field and he could not see the ball's flight path, he would say, 'The crowd noise will tell us if the kick is going to go over, so LISTEN! ... It's a goal!!!' The call became his trademark.

As a kid I used to go to Athletic Park and sit near the open broadcasting box, where I could watch him. He was thrilling to be around. I was there every week. The day he said 'Hi, sonny' was one of the great days of my youth.

And I'll let you into a secret – I've always wanted to do a

..it's
a
goal !

"RUGBY IN MY TIME"
by
Winston McCarthy
this week and every week in

THE NEW ZEALAND
LISTENER
ORDER YOUR COPY HERE

'LISTEN! ... It's a goal!!!' in a broadcast. If you hear me one day, you'll know it is a hark back to the man who got me started.

KEITH QUINN, *a leading New Zealand sports commentator, works for TV One Sport, where he began his career in 1973.*

BEST SNOWBOARD RUN

Cardrona Alpine Resort

Pamela Bell

For me, Cardrona has the best halfpipes, park, rails and boarder-cross course in the country. It also has the longest-standing relationship with snowboarders, and has supported snowboarding competitions and facilities right from the time snowboarding really started to take off in the early 1990s.

In one day at Cardrona you can work on tricks in the perfectly shaped halfpipes, take your choice from a range of rails and jumps for different abilities in the park, race down the boarder-cross course, riding the berms and woop-de-do's as fast as you can, and go off-trail in the Arcadia chutes, riding fresh tracks and steep, challenging lines.

And if all my dreams came to fruition at once, I would hop on a helicopter and fly to back-country terrain in the nearby Harris Mountains. Fresh tracks,

virgin snow, dry powder and a bunch of great mates – that's what snowboarding stories are made of.

PAMELA BELL *took up snow-boarding at the age of 18, and the following year won an event at the New Zealand national championships.*

She went on to win the nationals six years in a row. She competed on the World Cup circuit for four years and in 1998 became the first person to represent New Zealand in snowboarding at a Winter Olympics – in Nagano, Japan.

She has a degree in architecture and runs her own snowboard clothing company, Fruition snow-system.

BEST TELEVISION COMMERCIAL

'Dear John'

Bob Harvey

BOB HARVEY *founded McHarman Advertising in 1963. It rapidly became one of the first hotshot agencies, and won the first international award for New Zealand advertising. The agency became McHarman Ayer in 1990, and in 1992 was sold to Walkers Advertising. Harvey left the industry and was elected mayor of Waitakere City, a position he has held for nearly 12 years.*

I don't know anything that goes off quicker than TV commercials. Maybe fish. What was brilliant, stunning and award-winning last year is this year's corn, mixed with a little cement.

If there were a golden age when commercials changed the way we looked and thought, it was the 1970s. Commercials left the dull, grey studios, where housewives polished and glowed over windows and furniture, and discovered the great New Zealand outdoors. No one did it better than Nescafé, who even took the liberty of including Maori in their commercials.

But the best commercials came from the anti-fur brigade. On the catwalk, models swished by in furs revealing the blood and guts of dead animals. In fashion showrooms, flash dames selected furs whose interiors

dripped maggots. But these commercials were made in Britain, not New Zealand.

Television advertising here peaked in the 1980s. Clients demanded a great storyboard, fantastic talent and direction, and an extraordinary punch line. Amazing and exciting commercials were made, and New Zealand agencies were up there with the world's best. Steinlager, Toyota, Cadbury Crunchie bar and Trumpet ice creams made summer worthwhile. Boardroom shelves groaned with awards.

And the best of all was 'Dear John', directed by Tony Williams, in which a nerdy young American soldier in Vietnam gets dumped by his girlfriend via a tape recording, and its brilliant punch line: 'BASF – Even the bad times sound good.'

BEST CLASSICAL MUSIC FESTIVAL

Adam New Zealand Festival of Chamber Music

Lindis Taylor

LINDIS TAYLOR *is a music critic for* The Dominion Post.

In the world of classical music, festivals are where dreams are made. All over Europe, and increasingly in North America, such festivals flourish. People flock to them as they once did to Woodstock, and do now to Glastonbury.

At these festivals you find world-famous performers alongside young ones, in juxtapositions designed to amaze – and to provide fodder for later dinner-party boasting such as 'where I first heard the Gewürtstraminer Quartet play Ligeti'.

There's only one music festival of this ilk in New Zealand – the Adam New Zealand Festival of Chamber Music, which takes place every two years in Nelson. It's been going since 1992 and I've been to most of them since then.

A handful of wonderful, genial overseas artists come along,

chosen as much for their friendliness and joviality as for their musical talent. They play with New Zealanders in the fine Nelson School of Music – the oldest independent music school in the country, in the cathedral, in churches in nearby towns such as Motueka, Takaka and Blenheim, and in parks at lunchtimes.

The festival offers a voluptuous mixture of sun, laziness, drinking, swimming, walking, art-exploring – and twenty full days of music. Some of us could not live without it.

Goldner String Quartet

BEST TROUT FISHING SPOT

Tauranga—Taupo River

Bob Jones

Really there's no such thing as a best fishing spot. Rather there's a best combination of fishing factors: a stony-bottom river, shallow along one side, with a deep rift opposite, along which the trout lie. There are literally thousands of river stretches like this across New Zealand so, to be special, three further ingredients are necessary.

In order they are, first, that no other bastard is within ten miles of the spot. Isolation is the most endearing quality the angler seeks. The next requirement is that the stretch has heaps of trout lying in it. That's potluck, varying by the day. Finally, perfection requires a pleasant, balmy, windless day, in which the only disturbance is birdsong.

Most anglers have experienced such magical combinations, which induce a blissful euphoria unmatched by any other human experience. My most memorable happened over 30 years ago on the Tauranga–Taupo River. There were few anglers and the daily limit bag, unlike today's three, was an optimistic twenty trout.

I was trying to impress a girl. Having settled her on the riverbank with a book, and covered my back by explaining at length that it would be a miracle if I caught anything, I waded in and cast. Bang! Immediately I was into a rainbow. For the next three hours I played trout non-stop and took a limit bag.

The only black spot was the girl raging at me for this terrible cruelty. Explanations that she was witnessing a miracle, which she was, were dismissed as lies.

BOB JONES *is a novelist, non-fiction writer and property investor. He has been fishing for trout since 1961 and has caught several billion.*

BEST PIECE OF JEWELLERY

Sapphire, pearl and gold drop earrings

Jan Macdonald

JAN MACDONALD *is co-owner of Avid, a Wellington gallery founded eleven years ago to deal in applied arts. Her personal collection of ceramics, glass and art featured in the visitor programme of the 2004 New Zealand International Arts Festival.*

Wonderful jewellery can come from combining unusual elements with great sentimental value. In this case I gave Matthew von Sturmer sapphires from a ring my mother had left me and pearls from the Bosphorus, which I had bought in Turkey twenty years before. From these elements, he created earrings which are very elegant but also have a slightly wacky look.

In Avid, we come into contact with the work of many talented, imaginative and highly skilled New Zealand jewellery designers. People such as Paul Annear, Kobi Bosshard, Ann Culy, Peter McKay and Warwick Freeman produce work that is always beautiful, often astonishing.

Matthew von Sturmer is there with the best of them. He not only designs jewellery but also furniture, door handles, vases,

bowls and candlesticks.
He works in gold, bronze,
aluminium and timber. His

designs have an organic quality,
inspired by nature and New
Zealand's Pacific identity.

BEST HISTORIC PLACE

Oamaru

Gavin McLean

GAVIN McLEAN *is an historian at the Ministry for Culture and Heritage and the author of* 100 Historic Places in New Zealand. *His heritage guides to Oamaru and Dunedin have been published by University of Otago Press.*

Small it may be but Oamaru is the embodiment of settler capitalism, the architecture of prosperity and imperialism set in stone. And how quick it was! Most of it went from quarry to streetscape within a single generation, from Charles Traill and Henry France's wooden stores of 1858 to the collapse of the building boom in 1884.

Here, historian Erik Olssen observed, 'Oamaru's leaders celebrated, in gleaming white limestone, the triumphs of the pioneers and the certainty of progress through capitalism.'

The little town's architects deliberately gave this mushroom colonial whippersnapper the sense of permanence of an established European city many times its size, even if their ostentation frequently stretched no further than the facade. Oamaru still looks pretty much that way, thanks to long periods of recession and the main highway bypassing the old business district.

Twenty years ago locals rediscovered the value of the historic precinct and re-launched it under the theme 'Victorian Town at Work'. Now the Oamaru Whitestone Civic Trust owns a dozen fully restored heritage buildings, and the local district council and private owners have restored many more Victorian hotels, shops and grain stores.

There is a Heritage Week each November, a traditional boats' day each March, and Oamaru is the only place in New Zealand where penny-farthing bicycles form part of the daily traffic flow.

BEST CHARDONNAY

Kumeu River Chardonnay 1989

Sue Courtney

When I was first tasted Kumeu River Chardonnay 1989, after its release in 1990, it blew me away. I had never tasted New Zealand chardonnay like this before. And it was from Auckland! The following year this fabulous wine made by Michael Brajkovich went on to win the accolade of Best Chardonnay at the London International Wine Challenge.

Fourteen years on from vintage, it is still a classic example of the expression of this grape. It is a deep golden colour, befitting its age, with mellow, nutty oak, remnants of pineapple and citrus, a butterscotch richness, a warm, dry textural complexity and a honeyed character that comes with bottle-age. It was from a low-yielding vintage and was always a very fragrant, classy wine.

Over the years I have followed the development of Kumeu River Chardonnay and savoured the great vintages, such as 1991, 1996, 1998, 2000 – and 2002, in screw cap.

The single vineyard Kumeu River Maté's Vineyard Chardonnay was introduced in 1993. The 2002 vintage of this wine could be destined to be one of the greatest New Zealand chardonnays. I look forward to tasting it over the years to come.

SUE COURTNEY *fell in love with wine after tasting Cloudy Bay Sauvignon Blanc at the winery one sunny October morning in 1988. The pursuit of great New Zealand wine is now her passion. She writes for New Zealand and international publications and operates her own wine-dedicated website,* www.wineoftheweek.com.

BEST FEMALE IMPERSONATOR

Pollyfilla

Malcolm Kennedy-Vaughan

Pollyfilla (alias Colin McLean) is New Zealand's true queen of high camp – not only a talented female impersonator but a person who contributes much to many communities, and who crosses extreme boundaries to foster love and understanding.

Known throughout New Zealand, and indeed internationally, to people in all walks of life, Polly is always at the ready for charity fund-raisers and street collections. A memorable incident happened one year when she was collecting for the Aids Foundation on World Aids Day. She was standing on her usual corner outside a pharmacy in Wellington when a wealthy-looking gentleman in a BMW parked on broken yellow lines in order to pop in and pick up a prescription.

'Hey, you can't park there. That's illegal!' cried our diva. 'However, if you choose to make a worthy donation to my tin, I'll guard your car until you return.' To which the man duly replied, 'You're a good-looking lady and you have a good cause,' as he neatly folded a $100 note and slipped it in her tin.

Pollyfilla has won 'Queen of the Carnival' at Trentham Racecourse's *Fashion in the Field* three times. She performs in over 25 corporate shows a year, in Wellington's annual Fringe Festival and Summer City events, and at major gay and lesbian venues throughout the country. She still finds time to design and create astonishing costumes for herself and many other performers.

MALCOLM KENNEDY-VAUGHAN *has been actively involved in Wellington's gay community for the past 27 years. He and his partner, Scott Kennedy-Vaughan, own and manage the gay nightclub, Pound.*

BEST KAYAK RUN

Hokitika River

Mick Hopkinson

MICK HOPKINSON *was a member of the team that made first descents of the Inn River in Switzerland and Austria, the Blue Nile in Ethiopia, the Dudh Khosi in Nepal. He is co-director of the New Zealand Kayak School.*

I had narrowly missed out on the first descent of the Hokitika River. Graham Charles had instigated an exploratory frenzy for a new guide book, *100 Great Kayak Runs in New Zealand*, and I had joined his team. But the winds were too strong for the helicopter to battle up the gorge. Graham later completed the descent with another team: 'You should have been there. It was awesome.'

Finally, at the end of the 1999 season, I got my chance: I had a free day, the weather was good and long-time paddling partner Peter Kettering was available. We decided to go for it.

From the helicopter the river was a long series of gleaming white boulders, with thin, blue rivulets of water cascading over them. Punctuating the boulders were narrow slots so overhanging it was too dark to see into them. These were the famous gorges that gave the Hokitika its fierce reputation and had made the river inaccessible to all but kayakers.

Deposited on a sandy beach above some easy rapids, we nervously set off. Soon we were dropping down one waterfall after another, the rapids increasing in size and severity. The first gorge came up quickly, dark and foreboding. Once in it, retreat was impossible and it didn't take much imagination to see the courage Graham's team had had on the first descent.

In the end there were seven short gorges, every one a place where fear, adrenaline and river-sculpted rock created an almost spiritual atmosphere, akin to being in a great cathedral. A long, hard day brought us out to the confluence with the Whitcombe River and the finale back in the pub: 'You should have been there,' we raved. 'It was … awesome.'

BEST CRICKET GROUND

Willows Cricket Club

Don Neely

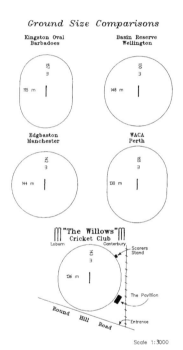

Ground Size Comparisons

Kingston Oval
Barbadoes

87 m

115 m

Basin Reserve
Wellington

150 m

148 m

Edgbaston
Manchester

142 m

144 m

WACA
Perth

165 m

130 m

"The Willows"
Cricket Club
Loburn   Canterbury

143 m

136 m

Scorers
Stand

The Pavilion

Round Hill Road

Entrance

Scale 1:3000

In North Canterbury, beyond Rangiora, on the way to Loburn, lies a cricket paradise. Down a gravel road, between huge shelter belts of macrocarpa, is the Willows Cricket Club. On a ground similar in size to the Basin Reserve, on a playing surface the equal of any first-class arena, secondary school First Elevens from around New Zealand play with and against mature players with test and first-class experience, learning the etiquette, manners and traditions of a game born in England in similar surroundings over 300 years ago.

Spectators laze on striped deck chairs under oversized canvas umbrellas. The northern reaches of the Southern Alps lie purple in the distance, with remnants of snow on the tops and in the gullies. The scent of grass, the wide space of sky above, the assorted greens of willow, gum,

poplar, macrocarpa and lime, the shrill caw of peacocks and the bleating of sheep all induce a drowsy sense of timelessness.

The game assumes the tone and colour of the surrounds. Players and spectators return from their visit with fresh understanding of the true spirit of cricket.

DON NEELY *has had a lifetime involvement with cricket as a player, historian and New Zealand selector for 14 years. Currently chair of the Board of Trustees of the New Zealand Cricket Museum, he is the author of* Men in White, *the definitive history of New Zealand cricket, and co-author of* The Basin: An Illustrated History of the Basin Reserve.

JENNIFER SHENNAN *is a
free-lance dance writer and reviewer
with special interests in European
dance history and the anthropology
of Pacific dance traditions.*
Dancers from left: Daniel Belton,
Mia Mason, Shona McCullagh, and
Sean MacDonald.

BEST DANCE WORK

Gloria

Jennifer Shennan

To Vivaldi's exuberant music, Douglas Wright has made a dance that, more than any other I have encountered, affirms and celebrates life. Gold-clad dancers launch themselves into the air and stay there, flying over each other in twists and plaits, bodies free from earth and weight, reaching for the stars but hitting the sun. Douglas was commissioned by his friend Helen Aldridge to make the work to commemorate the life of her daughter Deirdre Mummery, who had died tragically of a drug overdose. Douglas's work typically carries urgency and edge; in *Gloria* this is enhanced by the celebration of the life of a young woman. The embracing of every joyful, baroque quaver of the music shows what dance can do in the hands of a master choreographer.

BEST FREE ATTRACTION

Hot swim at
Kerosene Creek

Linda Duncan

Kerosene Creek is one of those magic places unique to New Zealand. I have lived my life only 55 kilometres away and yet until recently I never knew it existed.

To get there, drive 25 kilometres south from Rotorua on SH5 and then take the first road left after the turnoff to Murupara, on to Old Waiotapu Road. If you're coming from Taupo, drive 55 kilometres north on SH5 and turn off on to Old Waiotapu Road.

Don't look for any signs to lead you to this romantic spot as there are none. It is a short drive off the main road to the car park, where a two-minute walk leads you down a track to a spa-like pool, set among the bush and perfect for soaking weary bones. Further along the track there's a waterfall which has, at its foot, a pool large enough to swim in.

The temperature in Kerosene Creek varies and can cool after rain, but is generally about 35 to 39 degrees Celsius. When I discovered this place, I lay enveloped in warm water and thought, yes, the best things in life truly are free!

LINDA DUNCAN *is the author of* New Zealand for Free: North Island *and* New Zealand for Free: South Island. *Her passion for free activities was sparked when she noticed that the activities her family enjoyed and talked about most were the free ones.*

BEST STREET THEATRE

Urban Safari

Chris Morley-Hall

Night had fallen on the first day of the first-ever Cuba Street Carnival. The night parade was preparing to depart from the top of Cuba Street to bring the next spectacle to the crowds. I was coming up the centre of the road, checking everything was in place, and buzzing out on the atmosphere and the large numbers of people who had come out for the event.

Suddenly a group of animals came charging towards me – a giant pack of hyenas, working off each other, lunging into the crowds and rummaging through rubbish bins. We were all left speechless. Where did this lot come from? What are they? This is totally crazy.

There is something fantastic about street theatre and its ability to unexpectedly transform your world for a matter of minutes and leave behind deep, creative and

joyous memories. This was the first outing of Gait Productions' now internationally renowned *Urban Safari*. The show presents invaluable information about the cantilerper and the kennelpig, two species of animal that were believed to have been extinct for thousands of years before being rediscovered by safari tour guide Dr Wes on a hunting expedition in the urban jungle. And if you believe that …

CHRIS MORLEY-HALL *has worked in festivals and circuses in Europe and Latin America, fire-eating, knife-throwing, whip-cracking, lassooing, clowning and juggling. In 1999 he founded the Cuba Street Carnival, now an annual event, and the following year launched Whooper Chopper beach carnivals and an International Busking Festival.*

BEST PRIVATE WALKING TRACK

Banks Peninsula Track

Wally Hirsh

Getting close to the land is a favourite pastime in this beautiful country. Having tramped icons such as the Routeburn, Milford, Kepler, Queen Charlotte and Waikaremoana, we went looking for new experiences. We became aware that farmers and other rural people were beginning to open their land to trampers. The first of these private tracks to attract us was the Banks Peninsula, which begins and ends in Akaroa.

Today there are more than twenty private tracks, from Great Barrier Island in the north to Tuatapere in the south, but the Banks Peninsula Track is still hard to beat. From the first night in a trampers' hut high above Akaroa Harbour, to the last at Otanerito Bay, the scenery is exhilarating.

The track traverses farmland and bush, past waterfalls, down

valleys, along the rugged coastline, continually lashed by the mighty Pacific, and through Hinewai Reserve, with its canopies of tall kanuka and majestic beech forest. Along the way you see an amazing array of sea birds, dolphins, seals and possibly even a whale. The accommodation at the end of each day is enchanting and surprising. The silence is to be savoured.

WALLY HIRSH, *tramper, tour guide, adventurer and environmentalist, is the author of* Hidden Trails: 21 Private Walking Tracks in New Zealand. *He has travelled widely in the Pacific and in many other countries, including Australia, Botswana and Thailand, and is also an emerging potter.*

BEST RUGBY FIELD

Carisbrook, Dunedin and Westpac Stadium, Wellington

Anna Richards

I have played rugby all over New Zealand and the world but two grounds really stand out – Carisbrook and Westpac Stadium, known to one and all as the Cake Tin.

I have played on Carisbrook several times but one occasion, when the Black Ferns played Australia as a curtain-raiser to the All Blacks' 1997 Bledisloe Cup match, was particularly memorable. Dunedin in the week leading up to a Bledisloe Cup match is an event in itself. Finally the big day dawned, cold but clear. Excitement was high as we warmed up. Then, suddenly, trouble struck: one of our players, who had a heart condition, collapsed minutes before we were due to go on the field.

When we finally ran out, with a replacement player hurriedly plucked from the benches, we

were greeted with an enormous cheer from the crowded embankment. This turned out to be the largest and most vocal crowd we had ever played in front of. This, together with the 45–nil win against the Aussies, and the post-match festivities made it a thrilling experience.

My fondest memory of the Cake Tin is of the first and only time the New Zealand Women's Sevens team has played in New Zealand – at the 2001 International Sevens tournament.

The women's final took place in between the guys' games. The party atmosphere created by a huge, partisan crowd made it unforgettable.

ANNA RICHARDS *made her debut with the Black Ferns in 1990 and has since played over 20 tests for New Zealand. She was a member of both World Cup-winning Black Ferns sides – 1998 and 2002 – and captained the New Zealand Women's Sevens team to success in Hong Kong and Japan in 2000 and 2001. She has also played professional rugby overseas.*

Westpac Stadium

BEST SHORT STORY

'An Affair of the Heart'

Graeme Lay

I was first given Frank Sargeson's story to read in 1960, when I was in the sixth form at Opunake High School. It is about the Crawleys, an impoverished, fatherless family, who live in a shack beside the sea, and the mother's obsessive love for her son Joe.

Just as startling as its plot was the fact that the setting was recognisable. A callow 16-year-old, I had no idea that the country in which I was born had its own writers. Until then all the literature I had read had been by English, Scottish, Irish and American writers. But 'An Affair of the Heart' mentioned things like pipis and baches and kumaras, which proved that the place this beautiful, terrible story was set in was New Zealand, a place that was part of my life too. This seemed like a marvel.

Little did I know that reading that story marked the very first step on my path to becoming a writer myself. Thirteen years later I was to meet Frank Sargeson, the mysterious genius who had given me 'An Affair of the Heart' and who became my literary mentor.

GRAEME LAY *is the author of seven novels and several works of non-fiction. Secretary of the Frank Sargeson Trust, he lives and writes in Devonport, Auckland. His latest book is* The Miss Tutti Frutti Contest: Travel Tales of the South Pacific.

BEST EXTREME SKI SLOPE

The Pinnacles, Mount Ruapehu

Simon Wi Rutene

SIMON WI RUTENE *has represented New Zealand at four Winter Olympics and was named Skier of the Year in 1987 and 1988. He is a director of Hana Ltd, which encourages Maori economic development through education and information.*

On the southern margin of the volcanic plateau lies a group of volcanoes, Tongariro, Ngauruhoe and Ruapehu, gifted to the government in 1887 by Tuwharetoa chief Te Heu Heu Tukino. Mount Ruapehu, a huge, eroded volcano, is the highest point in the North Island. Its summit is permanently filled with ice, from which small glaciers flow down the mountainside.

The Skyline Ridge is situated on Ruapehu's north-western slopes, above Whakapapa skifield. It can be reached only by a 30-minute climb. However the adventurer is rewarded with a breathtaking downhill view of the awe-inspiring Pinnacles, or Nga Niho Taniwha, the taniwha's fangs.

At 2220 metres, Skyline is the ideal staging point for routes on both sides of the Pinnacles. Great caution is required. At any stage

here you can be confronted with life-threatening peril. Conditions can range from winter-blue, boiler-plate ice to fresh-melt spring corn on a rotten pack. Fresh powder may avalanche, and heavy, wet slush slurries need to be avoided. Both can, and often do, claim the lives of the unwary.

On the first part of the descent you encounter a razorback ridge, leading to the cavity from where the superior Pinnacles' south-west-facing chutes and couloirs are accessed. To manoeuvre into the twin coronets, where this steep, unrateably-extreme terrain commences, demands precision.

Crampons and ice axe need to be within quick reach.

These top routes of the Pinnacles exit at the mid-face, where there are several options – the seldom-done, terror-filled traverse to the pristine routes above the Pinnacle platter lifts, or the wonderful inner sanctum chutes, which terminate in serene Broken Leg Gully.

I revere Ruapehu, and the experience of mastering its extreme routes verges on the sublime. A grand sense of the paramount is to be found beneath the heavens and amidst the volcanic peaks. Connecting with such a sense is sacred. Hui e Taiki e.

BEST MASSAGE

Thai Yoga massage

Tania Greig

Asked for the best, a vision of a week of endless massages filled my mind. Should I go for the calm and warmth of the Balinese Hot Stone massage? Or perhaps a tension-releasing, therapeutic sports massage? In the end, though, I voted for Corey McInnes's energising two-hour treatment.

Traditional Thai Yoga massage – taught to Corey by global guru Asokananda – works on re-aligning the body's energy systems to remove emotional blockages and improve energy flow. As the work is done through the physical body, you also experience improvements such as increased blood flow, lessened muscle tension and increased flexibility.

The massage, which takes place on a futon on the floor with dim light and soft music, begins with Corey 'clicking' your toes. Thais believe that toe-clicking increases oxygen to the joints and prevents diseases such as arthritis. Then there is a half-hour of palm and thumb pressure to feet and legs, followed by leg-stretching.

At this point the treatment really begins to get interesting as Corey works on the stomach, arms and hands with all manner of unusual twists and manoeuvres. This form of healing is not for the faint-hearted; you must be willing to relax and allow the therapist to contort your body into some rather intimate positions.

After a few more stretches you will feel as though your body is slowly unlocking itself. The finale is a complete facial massage. You leave feeling truly alive.

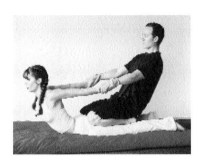

TANIA GREIG *is the founder and publisher of* Fitness Life *and* Kids Life *magazines. She has had over 20 years' experience in the health and fitness industry, ranging from clinical psychology to instructing fitness classes.*

BEST NEWSPAPER

The New Zealand Herald

Jim Tully

JIM TULLY *is head of the School of Political Science and Communication at the University of Canterbury. He worked in daily newspapers for eighteen years, becoming assistant editor and editorial manager of the* Auckland Star, *editor of the* 8 O'Clock *and inaugural New Zealand Journalist of the Year.*

She used to be dismissed as Granny Herald, a staid journal of record that lacked flair and imagination, a reluctant surfer on the wave of feminism, who long resisted the term Ms and held fast to a women's section – 'Mainly for Women' – long after such things were passé.

Now *The New Zealand Herald* – which includes a weekend edition, with a glossy magazine – is not just our biggest daily newspaper, but consistently the best. The new *Herald* is assertive, confident, and occasionally stroppy, with a much-improved design. It was always well-endowed with space and staff. Now it makes full use of them to give readers news that matters and in-depth background to make sense of it.

How did this transformation come about? Largely through new ownership, and the appointment of younger editorial executives willing to initiate change.

The New Zealand Herald

Auckland edition · Monday, September 1, 2003

Monday - Friday **$1.20**
Standard subscription. $1/week (GS tax may apply)

This lake is dying

THREATENED: Scientists say Lake Rotoiti is "a real mess" and is in danger of collapse if urgent action is not taken to solve the problem of man-made pollution generating algal blooms in its waters.
PETER / ALAN GIBSON

Time runs out for scenic treasures

ENVIRONMENT: Plea for Government aid in 'national disaster'

by Jo-Marie Brown

Scenic lakes in the central North Island are dying, and the Government is under growing pressure to find a solution to the crisis.

The state of Rotorua's sick lakes has prompted a top-level report to the Government on whether a new rescue plan is needed.

Environment Minister Marian Hobbs has already stepped in to try to stop the spread of toxic blue-green algae at Lake Tikapa.

This week, her ministry will tell her whether more Government action is needed to save the lakes from algal blooms, which make

water unsuitable for fish and unsafe for swimming.

Toxins in the water can cause illness in the liver and nervous system as well as skin rashes, hay fever and asthma attacks.

Scientists have been warning since the 1980s that some of New Zealand's most beautiful and popular lakes, such as Rotoiti, are threatened by human activities and byproducts such as farming and sewage.

Lake Rotoiti is now described by scientists as "a real mess".

They say it is in danger of collapse unless the amount of nitrogen and phosphorous entering the water from sources such as septic tanks,

animal wastes and fertiliser is immediately reduced.

In the past few months it has also emerged that:

■ The average size of trout caught in Rotoiti has dropped from 3kg in the mid-1990s to 2kg last summer.

■ Rotorua residents could face expensive bills for a new reticulated sewerage system to protect the district's lakes from further damage.

■ Farmers around Lake Taupo face a possible "nitrogen cap" which could limit stock numbers, especially cattle.

■ Other lakes around the country are expected to face similar problems within the next few years.

Environment Ministry chief executive Barry Carbon, who chaired Rotorua last month to see the problem for himself, told the Herald time might be running out for Lake Rotoiti and immediate assistance from the Government might be needed.

But he has played down local expectations of more help for the other lakes in the area – including Rotoehu, Okareka and Rotorua – saying local councils seemed to have action plans and had not asked the Government for help.

One group wanting Government aid is the LakesWater Quality Society, chaired by former National Party MP Ian McLean.

"The real question is how many lakes have to fall over before central Government decides it should take some action?" he said.

"It's now gone beyond a local issue and in our view it's a national environmental disaster."

Mr McLean and Rotorua's lakes were the first to suffer such a major decline in water quality, but other lakes such as Taupo and Waikohu would follow suit.

"They're just bigger and deeper but the same problems will eventuate. Act now there too. It'll just take a while longer."

Marian Hobbs visited the lakes in July and the Government would join efforts to help improve Lake Taupo's water quality.

Taupo is healthier than the Rotorua lakes but is showing similar

signs of deterioration.

The Government's decision upset many Rotorua residents, who felt their lakes were being ignored.

OUR DYING LAKES

Today the **Herald** begins a five-part series examining the environmental problems of some of our most beautiful lakes and the possible solutions.

SEE ALSO
'I was thinking, God, what's happened to the beautiful lake.'
— A Lake Rotoiti resident, A2

TOMORROW: Lake Rotorua.

ago, Mr Carbon told the Herald that four years of planning had led to the Lake Taupo partnership.

Efforts to restore the lake water quality there were simply further advanced than they were in Rotorua.

"Taupo is also a question of trying to fix the situation before it's broken," he said. "The lakes in Rotorua are already pretty sick."

Mr Carbon has admitted that until recently, his ministry was not aware of the extent of the problem.

The National Party's spokesman on the environment, Dr Nick Smith, has described the lakes' condition as "an environmental disaster".

He told Parliament's environment committee that the Government was wasting millions of dollars on policy advice instead of getting to and fixing the pollution problems.

Bourne speeding: other driver

by Natasha Harris

Rally ace Possum Bourne was driving on a straight road at more than 100km/h before his fatal accident, says the other rally driver involved in the collision.

Mike Barltrop of Queenstown spoke yesterday to the Herald as police wrapped up their investigation into the crash in the Cardrona Valley on Good Friday.

Bourne and his and co-driver

Chris Ruane were taking a familiarisation run on the hill-climb course when they came to a blind bend.

"I just saw this car coming out of nowhere braking heavily and I took evasive action.

"I sure as hell didn't expect something to come flying over the corner, over the brow at full speed."

Asked if Bourne was driving at more than 100km/h, Mr Barltrop replied: "Yes. It was just over a blind brow anyway."

Barltrop said he was travelling between 40 and 30km/h.

Other drivers had said Bourne might have been driving at 140km/h.

Both drivers took evasive action in the same direction.

"There was really one option," Barltrop said, "because there was a drop to one side and the bank on the other, so I tried to accelerate to the bank, the safe side."

Barltrop said that if the accident had happened today, he would have

taken the same actions.

"We're confident of a favourable [police accident investigation] report I think it will all be over then."

The police expect to finish the report by Tuesday next week.

Bourne's widow, Peggy, declined to speak to the Herald. A family member said the police had withdrawn her not to talk to the media.

Bourne died on April 30 after life support was withdrawn. Barltrop's leg was badly broken in the accident.

Anger at streaker dare

The Canterbury Rugby Union has been told two streakers at its Ranfurly Shield game may have been trying to win a bike raced dare by former All Black Marc Ellis.

The naked men were arrested on Saturday night as they tried to get onto the ground during the Canterbury-Taranaki match at Jade Stadium. It is understood a young girl was knocked over in the melee.

Christchurch police are angry that the incident may have been provoked by Ellis live on TV3's Sports Cafe.

Host Ric Salizzo said he tried to retract the dare, but his officials was adamant.

"We did point out on the show that we don't promote or condone streaking in any way. Marc may see it differently. He made the call then I, as a responsible person, said, 'We are responsible people and can't condone that'. Ric Hills said, 'Shut up, I do or something along those lines."

Salizzo said any payout was to be based on the number of security guards a streaker managed to sidestep once on the playing surface.

• SEE ALSO
Rugby coverage – Sport, C13

KICKED OUT: A streaker is hustled out of the stadium.

BEST RECORDED SONG

'Point That Thing Somewhere Else'

Chris Knox

The best song in the history of New Zealand recorded music is, despite what anyone else may say, 'Point That Thing Somewhere Else' by The Clean. It speaks of paranoia but ends in the most gloriously cathartic, three-chord outro that sings of the power, the glory and flying into the very centre of the sun.

Many a fine hallucination has accompanied the song's majestic mutations. Many a relationship has started in the many-tentacled grip of its sinuous sonorities. I daresay many a young life has begun as its last notes faded from the bedroom stereo. Seldom have so few chords moved so many so deeply.

The song has always been in the band's live set and has taken a myriad of forms over the nearly twenty-five years they have been playing the beautiful thing. But the prototype, inevitably, has become

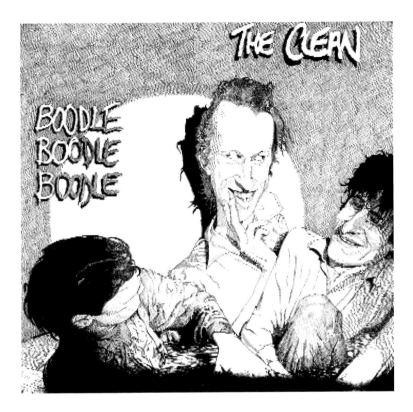

the first recorded version on
their life-changing *Boodle Boodle
Boodle* Flying Nun EP.

CHRIS KNOX, *despite what anyone
else may say, is a wildly overrated hack
of all trades, up to his neck in multiple
cartooning deadlines and trying to write
the odd (very odd, some would say)
song. Too old to be of much use to
anyone, he is still open to suggestions.*

BEST MOUNTAIN BIKE RIDE

Queen Charlotte Track

Simon Kennett

For me, as an old-school mountain biker, adventure and stunning scenery are critical ingredients for a great ride. The Queen Charlotte Track in the Marlborough Sounds offers generous portions of both, and much more – history, native birdlife and the chance to meet friends old and new.

The trip starts in Picton with a water taxi trip out to Ship Cove, one of Captain Cook's landing spots. After being harangued by the local weka, it's off up the first climb, mostly too steep to ride but rewarded with a stunning vista at the summit and a hoot of a descent.

The track is narrow and hugs the side of a steep hill; it doesn't take much speed to feel you're riding on the edge.

At almost 80 kilometres, the Queen Charlotte is the longest 'single-track' in New Zealand. Following it one hundred percent is a challenge for fit, expert riders but for those in cruise mode there are a couple of opportunities to bypass the big hills in favour of the sealed, but still scenic, road.

The last section of the track, to Anakiwa, is a must-do for all riders. Well-graded, it passes through beautiful beech forest and climaxes with an exhilarating downhill. If the sun's shining, this is the spot to jump in the sea, have a picnic on the grass, and pause to reflect how sweet life can be.

SIMON KENNETT *has been riding and racing bicycles for over twenty years. He is co-author of* Classic New Zealand Mountain Bike Rides, *now in its fourth edition.*

BEST RACECOURSE

Trentham Racecourse

Mary Mountier

I have to choose Trentham, even though, over the nearly half-century I've been going there, my wins-to-losses ratio has been appallingly low.

I was introduced to racing at Trentham when I was twelve. Given ten shillings to bet with, I picked a horse called Baraden. It came second. I won nearly five pounds. It was so exciting, and I felt so rich. Since then, though, I've found out why Trentham is called 'the punter's graveyard'.

Heavily influenced by two older brothers, whom I aspired to emulate, I found horse-racing a magical world I could share with them – and with my Irish-born mother, who loved a flutter all her life. When I grew older, I inveigled a variety of boyfriends into taking me to Trentham – then always a fashionable place to be seen – even if racing bored them silly.

What is it about horse-racing that fascinates us devotees? It's a sport full of paradoxes – at once exhilarating, dramatic, heart-warming … and tedious, repetitive and blood-chilling. It provides huge highs and lows to everyone, from owner to punter. It appeals to the best and worst of characters.

My most memorable moment was in 1963, watching the 10-year-old Great Sensation win his third Wellington Cup. From the top of the public stand I saw the huge crowd and heard the deafening roar as it became obvious the old champion was going to get up and win.

Twenty years later I was part of a syndicate with a horse in the Cup. Heartstopper ran only seventh but we didn't care. We were simply thrilled she had been good enough to get a start.

MARY MOUNTIER *has written six books about racing, including* Notable Thoroughbreds of New Zealand *and* Racing Women of New Zealand. *She became well-known in the 1980s as the sole female voice on the Radio Racing Show. Her book* How to Pick a Winner *will be published in 2004.*

Trentham Racecourse on the day of its
Golden Jubilee, January 1956.

BEST CHILDREN'S PICTURE BOOK

Slinky Malinki

John McIntyre

Lynley Dodd is that rarest of talents in children's literature – a writer who can illustrate, and an illustrator who can write. She is a major worldwide name in a genre crowded with famous names.

Dodd's creation Slinky Malinki is a wonderful character, a feline kleptomaniac, mischievous and contrite. The story bounces along with brilliant rhythm and rhyme.

The other hot contenders for best picture book are Margaret Mahy's *Dashing Dog* and *Summery Saturday Morning*. In these works, which feature delightful animal capers, Mahy is probably at her absolute peak. Her craft shines through in her ability to entertain through story. There is never a word too many, never a word wasted. And each book has been illustrated by world-class illustrators – Sarah Garland for *Dashing Dog* and Selina Young for *Summery Saturday Morning*.

JOHN McINTYRE *owns and operates The Children's Bookshop in Wellington, named New Zealand Independent Bookshop of the Year in 2003. A judge of the New Zealand Post Children's Book Awards in 1998/99, he also reviews children's books on National Radio's* Nine to Noon *programme.*

BEST FILM

Goodbye Pork Pie

Jane Wrightson

JANE WRIGHTSON *has been chief executive of the Screen Production and Development Association, chief film censor, deputy chief executive of New Zealand On Air and commissioning editor for Television New Zealand. In 2003 she was appointed chief executive of the Broadcasting Standards Authority.*

I'm a hoon from Hawke's Bay, a dying breed if one buys into the current fuss about the great province where I was born and raised. We certainly weren't drinking wine back then, let alone making it, and we didn't take much seriously, especially authority. So my pick for best New Zealand film is not the most technically splendid (that'd be the *Rings* juggernaut), nor the one that made me laugh and cry the most (*Whale Rider*). It's not the most prophetic (*Sleeping Dogs*), nor the most beautiful (*Illustrious Energy*), nor even the one which made me see my country differently (*Ngati*).

Nope, my best film is one that even the director thinks is merely good, not great. Geoff Murphy's *Goodbye Pork Pie* was perhaps the third New Zealand film I ever saw. A year or so out of university, I'd been touched by virtually no New Zealand culture en route. Suddenly the little yellow Mini exploded out of nowhere with the silliest, most anarchic story imaginable. On the big screen I saw the street I lived in, heard dialogue and slang I'd only ever heard at parties up home, and witnessed outrageously stupid car-and-cop chases that left me crying with laughter. I'd have slapped the bimbo (those film blokes never could write female characters), but I really wanted to be Kelly Johnson.

And we made it here! For the first time I understood that there might be stories to be proud of in this film industry lark.

It was also the last time for a while we laughed together as a nation. The 1981 Springbok tour started a few months later and everything changed.

BEST MOUNTAIN CLIMB
South Face of Mount Hicks
Graeme Dingle

Often one is drawn to climb a mountain by its beautiful shape, but in the case of Mount Hicks it was the awesome reputation of its south face that committed Murray Jones and me to the challenge. We had never seen the face, as the mountain is tucked around behind the highest of them all, Aoraki, but we knew it was regarded as one of the last great unclimbed ones in the Southern Alps.

So, on the last day of 1970, Murray and I crunched across the frozen surface of the Sheila Glacier, as the wall of Hicks' south face rose ominously over us – through shadowy vertical buttresses to the summit's ice-cliffs, glowing golden in the early light.

Our route ascended the very centre of the wall, following a fine rib of red rock. Pitch by pitch, we performed our eccentric vertical dance. In the fading light we

climbed the last steep ice to the summit, as a cry of appreciation went up from climbers watching from the tiny dot that was the hut far below. Now like wild animals, we searched under the livid green sky for a ledge on which to spend the night.

Descending the next day, we were stopped in the valley by an old man who reminded me of the Ancient Mariner. 'Why do you call it Hicks?' he asked me. 'Its real name is St David's Dome, after the dome of a cathedral in Europe. Those bastards in Wellington changed its name!' he thundered.

GRAEME DINGLE *has achieved hundreds of mountaineering, rock-climbing and adventuring firsts, including the first ascent in one season of all six classic European north faces, first traverse of the Southern Alps, first traverse of the Himalaya, and a 400-day, 28,000-kilometre circumnavigation of the Arctic. The author of ten books, he is the founder of the Sir Edmund Hillary Outdoor Pursuits Centre and the Project K Trust.*

BEST SURF BEACH
Mangamaunu, Kaikoura
Gary McCormick

This is a beautiful right-hand point break. Which in surfing terms is a long, perfect wave. Backdrop of snow-capped mountains, and numerous sharks. Excellent!

GARY McCORMICK *is a poet, entertainer, television performer, breakfast host on MoreFM radio and self-described ageing surfer.*

INDEX & CONTACTS

EXTREME SKI SLOPE *(page 90)*
The Pinnacles, Mt Ruapehu
Whakapapa Ski Field,
Ruapehu Alpine Lifts Ltd,
Private Bag, Mt Ruapehu,
tel (07) 892-3738, www.mtruapehu.com

FEMALE IMPERSONATOR *(page 70)*
Pollyfilla
Colin McLean, Pollyfilla Productions,
tel (04) 972-1000, 021-123-7543,
pollyfilla@hotmail.com

FILM *(page 106)*
Goodbye Pork Pie
New Zealand Film Commission,
PO Box 11-546, Wellington,
tel (04) 382-7680,
www.nzfilm.co.nz

FREE ATTRACTION *(page 78)*
Hot swim at Kerosene Creek

GOLF COURSE *(page 18)*
Kauri Cliffs Golf Course
Kauri Cliffs, Matauri Bay Road,
Matauri Bay, PO Box 800, Kerikeri,
tel (09) 407-0060,
www.kauricliffs.com
Paraparaumu Beach Links
Paraparaumu Beach Golf Club,
376 Kapiti Road, PO Box 1544,
Paraparaumu Beach,
tel (04) 902-8200,
www.paraparaumubeachgolfclub.co.nz

GREAT WALK *(page 34)*
Heaphy Track
Department of Conservation – Golden Bay
Area Office, 62 Commercial Street,
PO Box 166, Takaka, tel (03) 525-8026,
www.doc.govt.nz

HISTORIC PLACE *(page 64)*
Oamaru
Oamaru Information Centre,
1 Thames Street, Oamaru,
tel (03) 434-1656, www.tourismwaitaki.co.nz;
Oamaru Whitestone Civic Trust,
2 Harbour Street, Oamaru,
tel (03) 434-1406, www.historicoamaru.co.nz

ICE CREAM *(page 6)*
Deep South Vanilla
Deep South Ltd, 122 Rockdale Road,
PO Box 1655, Invercargill,
tel (03) 216-5685, www.deepsouthnz.co.nz
Kapiti Fig & Honey
Kapiti Fine Foods, 57 Te Roto Drive,
PO Box 122, Paraparaumu,
tel (04) 297-0329, www.kff.co.nz

INDEPENDENT CINEMA *(page 30)*
The Paramount
25 Courtenay Place, Wellington,
tel (04) 384-4080, www.paramount.co.nz

JAZZ ENSEMBLE *(page 12)*
Anthony Donaldson and The Village
Idiots
PO Box 11-816, Wellington,
tel (04) 385-1665

KAYAK RUN *(page 72)*
Hokitika River
Westland Visitor Information
Centre, Hamilton and Tancred
Streets, Private Bag 22, tel (03) 755-6166,
hkkvin@xtra.co.nz;
Tourism West Coast, www.west-coast.co.nz

KIWIANA *(page 28)*
Horopito Motors
Private Bag, Raetihi, tel (06) 385-4151,
www.horopitomotors.co.nz

MASSAGE *(page 92)*
Thai Yoga Massage, Corey McInnes
BodyTech Fitness and Spa,
16 Normanby Road, Mt Eden, Auckland,
tel (09) 623-3383, www.bodytech.co.nz

MOUNTAIN BIKE RIDE *(page 98)*
Queen Charlotte Track
Department of Conservation – Sounds Area
Office, 14 Auckland Street, PO Box 161,
Picton, tel (03) 520-3002,
www.doc.govt.nz;
Queen Charlotte Track (Incorporated),
www.qctrack.co.nz

MOUNTAIN CLIMB *(page 108)*
South Face of Mount Hicks
Department of Conservation –
Aoraki/Mount Cook National Park,
PO Box 5, Aoraki/Mt Cook,
tel (03) 435-1819,
www.doc.govt.nz

MUSIC VIDEO *(page 4)*
Stand Up, Scribe
Fish 'n' Clips, 14 Charlotte Street,
Eden Terrace, Auckland,
tel (09) 309-2394, www.fishnclips.com;
Director – Chris Graham, producer – James
Moore, cinematographer – Nic Finlayson,
song producer – P-Money

**NATIVE TREE FOR A SMALL
GARDEN** *(page 14)*
Ti Kouka, Cabbage Tree
McLean Landscapes, 18 Wallace Street,
Herne Bay, Auckland,
tel (09) 376-5955, 021-757-196,
www.mcleanlandscapes.co.nz

NEWSPAPER *(page 94)*
The New Zealand Herald
46 Albert Street, PO Box 32, Auckland,
tel (09) 379-5050, www.nzherald.co.nz

NOVEL *(page 48)*
Coal Flat by Bill Pearson
Heinemann, Auckland, 1976
(out of print, try your local library)

PARK *(page 22)*
Grey Lynn Park
Grey Lynn, Auckland; Auckland City
Council, 1 Greys Avenue,
Private Bag 92-516, Auckland,
tel (09) 379-2020, www.aucklandcity.govt.nz;
Grey Lynn Park Festival,
www.greylynnparkfestival.co.nz

SHORT STORY *(page 88)*
'An Affair of the Heart'
The Frank Sargeson Trust,
Graeme Lay, Secretary
50 Lake Road, Devonport, Auckland
tel (09) 445-6953, graemelay@xtra.co.nz

SNOWBOARD RUN *(page 54)*
Cardrona Alpine Resort
PO Box 117, Wanaka,
tel (03) 443-7341 (mountain),
(03) 443-7411 (Wanaka),
www.cardrona.co.nz

SPORTS COMMENTATOR *(page 52)*
Winston McCarthy

STREET THEATRE *(page 80)*
Urban Safari
Drew James, Gait Productions,
80C Main Road, Titahi Bay, Wellington,
tel 0274-589-552,
www.gaitproductions.co.nz

SURF BEACH *(page 110)*
Mangamaunu, Kaikoura
Kaikoura Information and Tourism,
West End, Kaikoura, tel (03) 319-5641,
www.kaikoura.co.nz

TELEVISION COMMERCIAL *(page 56)*
'Dear John'
Tony Williams Productions: Director – Tony
Williams, producer – Bruce Smythe, writer –
Roger Brittenden. Tony Williams: Sydney
Film Company, www.sydneyfilm.com.au

TROUT FISHING SPOT *(page 60)*
Tauranga–Taupo River
Fishing licence essential; www.doc.govt.nz/
explore/hunting-and-fishing/taupo-fishery

ACKNOWLEDGEMENTS

The publisher acknowledges the kind permission of copyright holders in allowing reproduction of their illustrations in *Best: A New Zealand Compendium.*

ADRENALINE RUSH
Photograph: Geoff Mackley

MUSIC VIDEO
Photographs: Fish 'n' Clips

ICE CREAM
Photographs: Kapiti Fine Foods & Deep South Ltd

DOC HUT
Photograph: Department of Conservation/ Te Papa Atawhai, Nelson Lakes National Park Collection, 2003

CAFÉ
Photograph: Ian Baker

JAZZ ENSEMBLE
Photograph: courtesy Anthony Donaldson

NATIVE TREE FOR A SMALL GARDEN
Photographs: Gil Hanly

PLAY
Photograph: Peter Dinnan, courtesy Bats Theatre

GOLF COURSE
Photographs: courtesy Paraparaumu Beach Golf Club; Kauri Cliffs Golf Course

BLUE CHEESE
Photographs: A. Alferink; *Franklin County News*

PARK
Photographs: courtesy Auckland City Council; illustration courtesy Grey Lynn Park Festival

REGGAE BAND
Album cover: Dread, Beat & Blood, *Tribute to a Friend*, courtesy Jayrem Records

BEER
Photograph: Jane & Andrew Dixon

KIWIANA
Photographs: Mark Harris

INDEPENDENT CINEMA
Photograph: James Gilberd, Photospace

POEM
'Home Thoughts' by Denis Glover: poem courtesy Estate of Denis Glover; photograph courtesy Alexander Turnbull Library

GREAT WALK
Photographs: S. Frimmel, Department of Conservation/Te Papa Atawhai

PINOT NOIR
Illustration: Fromm Winery

ALBUM BY A SOLO ARTIST
Album cover: design by Terence Eady

DIVE SPOT
Photographs: Wade Doak; Seafriends Marine Conservation and Education Centre

RADIO BREAKFAST SHOW
Photograph: courtesy Radio New Zealand

BOUTIQUE HOTEL
Photograph: courtesy Awaroa Lodge

NOVEL
Book cover: from *Coal Flat*, Heinemann, Auckland, 1976

PRIVATE GARDEN
Photograph: Bev McConnell

SPORTS COMMENTATOR
Illustration: from *New Zealand Listener*, 1958, courtesy Alexander Turnbull Library, National Library of New Zealand/Te Puna Matauranga o Aotearoa

SNOWBOARD RUN
Photograph: courtesy Cardrona Alpine Resort

TELEVISION COMMERCIAL
Photograph: Sal Criscillo, courtesy Tony Williams Productions

CLASSICAL MUSIC FESTIVAL
Photograph: *Nelson Mail*

TROUT FISHING SPOT
Photograph: Denis Robinson

PIECE OF JEWELLERY
Photograph: Haru Sameshima

HISTORIC PLACE
Photographs: Gavin McLean

CHARDONNAY
Photographs: courtesy Kumeu River Wines

FEMALE IMPERSONATOR
Photographs: Malcolm Kennedy-Vaughan; *The Dominion Post*

KAYAK RUN
Photograph: Graham Charles, Image Matters Photography

CRICKET GROUND
Photograph: Don Neely

DANCE WORK
Photograph: Peter Molloy

FREE ATTRACTION
Photograph: Linda Duncan

STREET THEATRE
Photograph: Gait Productions

PRIVATE WALKING TRACK
Photograph: Doug Hood, Banks Peninsula Track

RUGBY FIELD
Photographs: Dave Burke; Peter Bush

SHORT STORY
Photograph: David Roberts, The Frank Sargeson Trust

EXTREME SKI SLOPE
Photograph: Chris McLennan, courtesy Ruapehu Alpine Lifts Ltd

MASSAGE
Photograph: Gerald Shacklock

NEWSPAPER
Front page: *The New Zealand Herald*